How Do You Say GOODBYE to an ELEPHANT?

Maggie Leaves Alaska

**Written and Illustrated
by Dianne Barske**

Book Design by: Denise Martin

Copyright © 2008 Text and Illustrations by Dianne Barske
- First Edition -

Library of Congress Catalog Card Number: 2008937143

ISBN 978-1-59433-088-9

Printed in China

Dedication

Caring – one of the best things that can happen in any community. And that's what Maggie created, so much caring. I think of her as a catalyst for that caring, a magnet drawing our concern. Whether an individual thought she should stay in Anchorage at our Alaska Zoo or be moved south to be with other elephants, the motivation for that stance was caring.

It seems right, therefore, to dedicate this book to the Anchorage community, a community that cared for its elephant. And now we can rejoice as a community in what has come to pass for Maggie – a safe transport and her place in an elephant community, PAWS in California.

It's a happy ending for Maggie, and for the tale told in this book.

Dianne Barske
Author and illustrator

One elephant – just one –
Stood near her zoo barn.
Maggie the elephant
Just one in our town.

"She needs other elephants,"
Said people who cared.
"Her life would be better
With other elephants –
shared."

"We love her here!"
Some earnestly did shout.

"She'd be better there,"
Other voices rang out.

The town was quite torn.
There was so much concern.
The best for the elephant –
For that we did yearn.

Should she stay – Or should she go?
What was best for our Maggie?
To stay here in our snow?

'Twas finally decided.
Maggie needed more sun,
To be with other elephants
And not be just one.

She'd been here for two decades.
It was hard to let go
Of Maggie the elephant
We'd all come to know.

So the zoo
held a party
To help say
goodbye.

"We'll miss you
– our Maggie,"
Many said
with a sigh.

Some wrote her a poem.
Some drew elephant art,
For Maggie the elephant
Who'd won over our heart.

First I missed Annabelle
And now I'll miss you.
I hope you're so happy.
In your new zoo.
                    –Lee

Maggie, Maggie
You're my friend
My love for you
will never end.
                    –Lisa

Dear Maggie, we'll miss you so.
I'm so sad to see you go.
                    –Ethan

We'll miss your ears
We'll miss your trunk
But I won't miss your house –
That really stunk.
                    –E.G.

Bye, bye Maggie,
Fly safe in the sky.
                    –Lindsey

We wanted you to play with the big red buoy
It really was meant for an elephant toy.
When away you flew in the big gray plane
The lonely red buoy was all that remained.
                    –Robbie

We watched as the zoo
Readied Maggie to fly
To warm California,
Many miles through the sky.

Maggie raised up her trunk
And twice trumpeted – loud.
As if bidding farewell
To the gathering crowd.

This was the big day –
Maggie tromped into her crate,
The crate put on an airplane.
What would be her fate?

She'd been cause
for such caring,
Been here many years.
"Please do well,
elephant, Maggie,"
we said through
our tears.

We waited for news
As the plane flew away.
Would we find Maggie well
At the end of this day?

?

Soon came several photos,
Maggie out in warm sun.
Four elephant companions –
Mara, Ruby, Lulu –

Another named Seventy–One!

We'd said our goodbyes
And expressed lots of care.
Now big smiles filled Alaska.
"Look – Maggie's doing well there!"

She's found a new home,
A warm place – some new friends.
But Alaska's love for our Maggie –
It's true – never ends.

THE END

(But not really –
our caring for Maggie goes on . . . .)

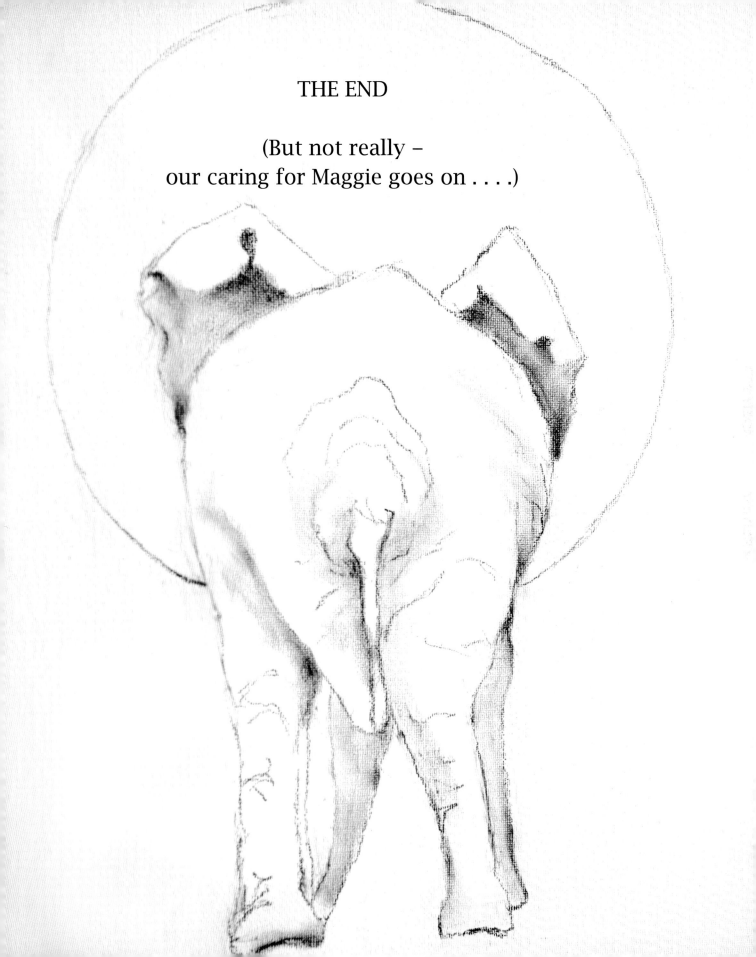

Maggie, Lulu, Mara, 71, and Ruby

photo by Janice Clark, PAWS photographer

Thank you, PAWS, for Maggie's new home.

PAWS, Performing Animal Welfare Society, is dedicated to the protection of performing animals, to providing sanctuary to abused, abandoned and retired captive animals, to enforcing the best standards of care for all captive wildlife, to the preservation of wild species and their habitats and to promoting public education about captive wildlife issues.

PAWS Web site:

www.pawsweb.org

WE CELEBRATE MAGGIE WITH ART

photo by D. Barske

For many years, children at the Alaska Zoo have had the opportunity to paint like an elephant – no hands – using a trunk mask and attached paint brush, supplied by Dianne and Elliott Barske. It's come to be known as Trunk Art, and has spread much joy and appreciation of the paintings of elephant artists like Annabelle and Maggie. Trunk Art was a special feature at Maggie's goodbye parties.

photo by J. Gomes

photo by J. Gomes

How Do You Say Goodbye to an Elephant?
Maggie Leaves Alaska

Maggie's History

How <u>do</u> you say goodbye to an elephant – a 25-year-old, 8,000-pound African elephant that Anchorage had come to know and love? When Anchorage bid farewell to Maggie in the fall of 2008, there were many individual and collective fond farewells. Many small children made goodbye cards for her and painted portraits of her on big murals at the Alaska Zoo. The zoo held a two-day, going-away party for Maggie, and the crowds came.

On November 1, 2008 Maggie flew south on an Air Force C-17 cargo plane. She tromped into her huge crate, made familiar to her by zoo keepers through weeks of training before she flew off to PAWS in California, an elephant sanctuary run by the Performing Animal Welfare Society.

Baby Maggie and Annabelle

Ironically, Maggie had been brought north as a baby elephant to the Alaska Zoo to provide companionship for another elephant, Annabelle, the Alaska Zoo's "matriarch." Many animal experts had pointed out that elephants are herd elephants, best not alone, and best in a warmer climate. When Annabelle died in 1997, Maggie was left alone.

Maggie traveled well on her long, 12-hour trip south, and now has four elephant companions – Ruby, Lulu, Mara and 71 – in her new California digs. Officials at PAWS have been pleased with Maggie's adjustment, and Maggie's concerned fan club in Anchorage breathed a huge sigh of relief. "Maggie is learning to be a California girl," officials at PAWS commented. "All the other elephants seem to like her." They added, "Maggie has waited many years for new companions and warm sunshine. We want her to enjoy her new home."

All of Anchorage, her old home, has the same wish.

THANK YOU

The author wishes to thank:

Eileen Floyd . . . . Alaska Zoo Development Director
Pat Lampi . . . . Zoo Director
John Gomes . . . . Zoo Photographer
Kim Gardner. . . . . PAWS Communications Director
Emilie Stout. . . . . granddaughter and IT specialist
Denise Martin. . . . . Layout and Design
Evan Swensen. . . . . Publisher
Anchor Lutheran School Early Childhood Program
and:
The children artists and poets whose goodbye images and thoughts are shared here, and everyone who came to Maggie's goodbye parties, showing us all "How do you say goodbye to an elephant."

photo by E. Barske

About the
author

Dianne Barske, artist and author, has lived in Alaska for 34 years.
She has written and illustrated two other books about animals at the
Alaska Zoo - both award-winners: *Mukluks for Annabelle* and *Two
Bears There, The Story of Ahpun and Oreo.*

Dianne teaches art to children and finds that a great adventure.
The American Diabetes Association has chosen her work three
times in a national Holiday Art Search competition for its annual
holiday cards. She is the mother of three and grandmother of two.
"Granddaughter, Emilie, was my technical assistant on this new
book," she states, "getting words and art into our computer."

WHAT AM I?

I have over 40,000 muscles in me.

I can store lots of water – 15 quarts at once.

I can pick up a tiny peanut or a big red beach ball.

I can hold a paintbrush.

I can spray a shower of dust or water.

I can scare off danger and am strong enough to rip the branches off a tree.

I can make an enormous trumpet sound – and –

When I sense friendliness, I can give a hug.

I am Maggie's trunk!

Pretend you have a trunk.

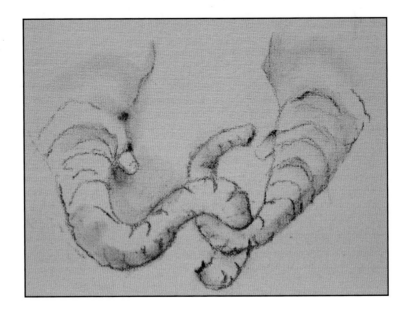

Peanut Gallery

Children's original artwork inspired by Maggie

used with permission